W9-BYH-547

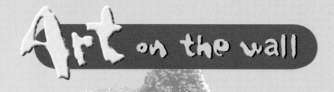

POP ART

Richard Spilsbury

Heinemann Library
Chicago, Illinois

© 2009 Heinemann Library
a division of Pearson Inc.
Chicago, Illinois

Customer service 888-454-2279
Visit our website at www.heinemannraintree.com

Produced for Heinemann Library by
White-Thomson Publishing Ltd
Bridgewater Business Centre
210 High Street, Lewes
East Sussex BN7 2NH, U.K.

Edited by Ruth Nason and Megan Cotugno
Designed by Mayer Media Ltd
Picture research by Amy Sparks and Ruth Nason
Originated by Chroma Graphics
Printed and bound in China by Leo Paper Products

13 12 11 10 09
10 9 8 7 6 5 4 3 2 1

Library of Congress Cataloging-in-Publication Data
Spilsbury, Richard, 1963-
  Pop art / Richard Spilsbury.
      p. cm. -- (Art on the wall)
  Includes bibliographical references and index.
  ISBN 978-1-4329-1368-7 (hc)
  1. Pop art--Juvenile literature. I. Title.
  N6494.P6S65 2008
  709.04'071--dc22

                              2008020358

Acknowledgments
Alamy **p. 16-17** (Pictorial Press Ltd); Pauline Boty
p. 14; Bridgeman Art Library **pp. 13** (Musée National d'Art Moderne, Centre Pompidou, Paris, France © DACS, London 2008), **19 top** (Pallant House Gallery, Chichester, U.K./The Estate of Patrick Caulfield. All rights reserved, DACS 2008), **26** (Whitney Museum of American Art, New York, © Jasper Johns/VAGA, New York/DACS, London 2008), **27** (Moderna Museet, Stockholm, Sweden, © DACS, London/VAGA, New York 2008), **29** (with permission from Claes Oldenburg. Musée National d'Art Moderne, Centre Pompidou, Paris, France, Peter Willi), **35** (Royal Academy of Arts, London, U.K.); Corbis **pp. 5** (Roger Wood), **7** (William Gottlieb), **8** (Rudolph Burckhardt/Sygma), **9** (© Succession Marcel Duchamp/ADAGP, Paris and DACS, London 2008), **10** (Hulton-Deutsch Collection), **13** (Ed Kashi), **28** (© The George and Helen Segal Foundation/DACS, London/VAGA, New York 2008), **33** (Christie's Images), **39** (Thinkstock); Chris Fairclough **pp. 18, 22 top, 23, 31, 38**; iStockPhoto **pp. 19 bottom, 22 bottom, 24 left**; Claes Oldenburg/Robert McElroy **p. 30**; Richard Pettibone **p. 21**; Shutterstock **pp. 15** (Karoline Cullen), **24 right, 37 & title page** (Cornel Achirei); Tate Images **p. 11** (© Trustees of the Paolozzi Foundation, Licensed by DACS 2008); Topfoto **pp. 4** (© The Estate of Roy Lichtenstein/DACS 2008), **25**; WT-Pix **p. 34**.

Cover photograph: Eduardo Paolozzi, *Wittgenstein in New York* (1965), Bridgeman Art Library (Sir E. L. Paolozzi/Pallant House Gallery, Chichester, UK/DACS)

The Publishers would like to thank John Glaves-Smith for his invaluable help in the preparation of this book.

Every effort has been made to contact copyright holders of material reproduced in this book. Any omissions will be rectified in subsequent printings if notice is given to the Publishers.

Contents

Some words are printed in bold, **like this.** You can find out what they mean by looking in the glossary.

What is Pop Art?

The picture on the wall below looks like part of a comic strip, blown up to a large size. The faces are painted with dots, similar to what you would see if you looked through a magnifying glass at a comic strip printed in a newspaper. But this isn't a section of a real cartoon. It is a painting from 1962 by the American artist, Roy Lichtenstein. He made it in the style of a cartoon, to echo popular images that people saw everyday in comics and newspapers. Art based on popular modern images was first created in the middle of the twentieth century by Lichtenstein and other artists. They are called Pop artists.

Art for the people

Pop Art is the name given to art focusing on popular **culture**, which was created from the middle of the 1950s until the end of the 1960s, in the United States and Britain. Pop artists generally chose **subjects** for their work that would be familiar to everyone. They made pictures and sculptures of certain types of things that people might see every day in the modern world around

Roy Lichtenstein was the first artist to paint images just like those in comics that were popular in the United States in the 1950s. This work, from 1962, is called *Masterpiece*.

4

This is Broadway, New York, in the 1960s. Many Pop artists were inspired by the bright, persuasive art of street advertisements and other popular images.

them, from household products, such as soup cans and popcorn, to banknotes, gas stations, road signs, and flags. They also represented subjects frequently seen in newspapers and magazines, on TV, or in movies, such as actors, singers, gangsters, cowboys, and cartoon characters.

Pop style

There is no one style of Pop Art. Some Pop artists, such as Lichtenstein, used smooth **brushstrokes** and areas of flat color to mimic the style of art seen in many printed advertisements and comics. Some artists, such as Andy Warhol, printed many images of movie stars or food packaging on canvas. Others, such as Robert Rauschenberg, painted somewhat messily with thick brushstrokes. What all Pop artists did share was a belief that their art should show the modern society in which they lived, and not the past.

Art movements

In the history of art, there are many periods of time when groups of artists created art with similar subjects, style, or inspiration. These phases in art are described as **movements**. Pop Art and **Impressionism** are examples of art movements. It is easiest to group artists together into a movement when looking back. At the time, artists were working individually, sometimes in different places, and did not try to copy each other. They may not have considered themselves part of a movement. With hindsight, we distinguish movements, in order to make sense of the development of art.

A New Movement

Why did Pop Art develop in the 1950s? What was going on in the world at that time? Although many countries in Europe took some time to recover after the end of World War II in 1945, by the 1950s, the United States and the United Kingdom were entering a new period of prosperity. This brought with it many social changes, which kick-started the new Pop movement in art.

Postwar changes

By the mid-1950s, the United States and the United Kingdom were becoming **consumer societies**. Industries were expanding fast. The rapidly growing populations had more money to spend, and so were buying more goods than ever before for themselves, their families, and their homes. The aim for many people was to be modern and up-to-date. In the 1950s, people bought bigger cars, televisions, new designs of furniture, and battery-powered razors, for example. Disposable items, such as ballpoint pens, designed to be thrown away after a few uses, came into the stores for the first time.

People also started to buy food that was different from that available in wartime. The new food required less or no preparation before eating, and included fast foods, such as hamburgers and frozen TV dinners in packages. This wider range of products could now be bought all together in bigger and bigger supermarkets, rather than from lots of individual stores.

The rise of art for businesses

With more people buying more things, companies competed for trade. They needed people with art skills to create **commercial art**. This included designs for products, and advertisements to entice customers to buy the products. Advertising was not new, but after the war, as companies tried to capture more sales, brand names and recognizable images became more important than before. Many brands were stacked together in supermarkets, and ads were not only on billboards and hoardings, but also in colorful magazines and on television.

Before the 1950s, artists who worked in advertising and design had usually started by following a traditional course of art study at art school. This involved, for example, learning oil painting techniques based on old masters (great artists of the past). In the 1950s, new art schools were opened specifically to train people to work as **graphic designers**, without following traditional art courses. These people would then be ready for careers in commercial art.

Memorable words

In the new consumer society of the 1950s, people wanted a convenient life, from supermarkets that stocked all types of goods, to prepared dinners straight from the freezer. Commercial artists were needed to design advertisements and packaging for such products.

In the 1950s, advertisers raced to develop short, snappy slogans to put alongside images to make consumers remember their products. Some famous slogans from this period are:

- *Does she... or doesn't she?* (Clairol hairspray, 1957)
- *Good to the last drop.* (Maxwell House coffee, 1959)
- *Melts in your mouth, not in your hands.* (M&Ms chocolate candies, 1954)

Art before Pop, in the United States

From around 1942 and through the 1950s, just before and as Pop Art developed, the dominant art movement in the United States was **Abstract Expressionism**. Some Abstract Expressionist artists, such as Mark Rothko, painted large canvases saturated in layers of a few deep, rich colors. Others, such as Jackson Pollock, created "action art" by dripping, pouring, and smearing paint on canvas. The work was **abstract**, because it showed no obvious, realistic subjects. It was **expressionist**, because the artists were trying to express deep feelings.

The movement developed just after U.S. forces had become directly involved in World War II, following the bombing of the U.S. Navy fleet at Pearl Harbor in December 1941. This was when many Americans first had glimpses of the horrors of the war in Europe, and some artists thought that realistic art could not adequately express the turmoil they felt.

Anti-art

Some artists in the United States, who thought that Abstract Expressionism was difficult to understand, were developing in a different direction. Allan Kaprow and Robert Rauschenberg, for example, were more excited by what happened when art was being made, than by a finished painting or sculpture. In the late 1950s, Kaprow organized **Happenings**, art events in which the audience took part. In some Happenings, artists created pieces out of anything, from chairs and food to smoke and old socks. In others, artists just did normal things, such as shopping or sweeping the streets. What was vital to such **anti-art** was that the audience was reacting to the Happening at a particular time and place. Some Happenings by other artists, such as Red Grooms, were like strange plays. Audience members had scripts with directions for what they should do in the piece.

Happenings took place in galleries, but also on the street, in parking lots, and in other unlikely places. The anti-art movement was sometimes called Neo-Dada, because the artists' beliefs were similar to those of **Dada** artists of the 1920s.

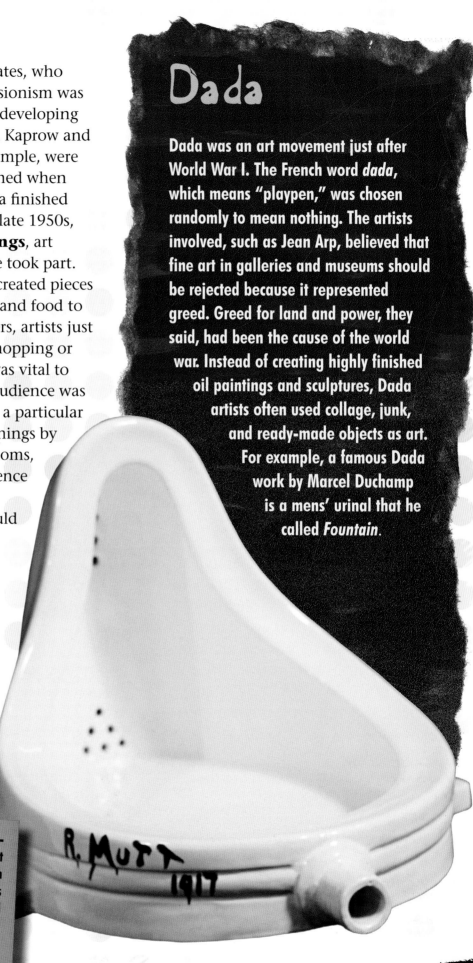

Dada

Dada was an art movement just after World War I. The French word *dada*, which means "playpen," was chosen randomly to mean nothing. The artists involved, such as Jean Arp, believed that fine art in galleries and museums should be rejected because it represented greed. Greed for land and power, they said, had been the cause of the world war. Instead of creating highly finished oil paintings and sculptures, Dada artists often used collage, junk, and ready-made objects as art. For example, a famous Dada work by Marcel Duchamp is a mens' urinal that he called *Fountain*.

Marcel Duchamp's *Fountain* was mass-produced in a factory, but became art when he exhibited it on its side in an art gallery. The signature "R. Mutt" was made up by Duchamp to hide his real identity. He knew *Fountain* would be very controversial!

Redefining British culture

In May 1951, the Festival of Britain began. At this time, many of Britain's cities were still in ruins after World War II, awaiting development. The festival was intended to give people a sense of recovery and patriotic pride, by celebrating British identity and industry. Exhibitions were held around Britain, and scientific inventions were displayed to show off Britain's achievements. The main exhibition was in newly built arts centers on the South Bank in London.

In 1952, a new British queen, Elizabeth II, came to the throne. Her coronation, in 1953, was another spur for an outpouring of patriotism and a celebration of Britain's history. Union Jack flags were flown all over the country.

At the same time, many young people wanted to redefine British culture, to make it reflect their modern interests and style more than the past. Young British artists, such as Peter Blake and Richard Hamilton, thought that popular images, including new car designs, photographs of models, pictures from science fiction comics, and scenes from movies, were more meaningful to most ordinary people than the traditional art found in museums and galleries. Hamilton said: *"Pop Art is popular, … low-cost, mass-produced, young, witty, sexy, gimmicky, glamorous, and Big Business."*

Looking west

American influences on European culture had grown during World War II and continued to spread afterward as the United States became a **superpower**. Contact with U.S. troops and seeing American magazines and news led more people in Europe to become interested in U.S. movie stars and music, including rock and blues. The United States was also seen in Europe as a classless society, in which any person could succeed by their skills and abilities. This was contrasted with traditional European societies, where success depended on being born into a wealthy family, with connections to people in power.

British artists became interested in American influences. Hamilton and others, including Eduardo Paolozzi, formed the **Independent Group**, which met at the new Institute of Contemporary Arts in London from 1952. They showed each other colorful images from American magazines and organized exhibitions of collages using some of these images.

The British artist, Eduardo Paolozzi, created a scrapbook of images called *Bunk!* from 1947 onward. Each page was a collage of images from U.S. magazines.

The first Pop Art?

Many people say that the first Pop Art piece was a collage by Richard Hamilton from 1956. It shows the interior of a modern home and is called *Just What Is It That Makes Today's Homes So Different, So Appealing?* Some people say that the first piece of Pop Art was a painting from 1955 by Peter Blake, called *On the Balcony*. This is a scene with four people on a bench, overlaid with popular images from magazines and newspapers and images of objects, including a can of sardines and a soda bottle.

The explosion of U.S. Pop

In the United States, popular commercial art had been seen on advertising hoardings and in magazines, comics, and newspapers for longer than in Britain, and artists had included commercial art images in their work quite early in the twentieth century. For example, in the 1920s, Stuart Davis painted a bottle of mouthwash as part of a still life. But in the 1950s, U.S. artists became interested in the meaning and importance of popular images as symbols—for example, of consumerism and industrial development. To make the symbols obvious, the artists presented them realistically, rather than transforming them in an artistic way.

Robert Rauschenberg and Jasper Johns are often considered the first U.S. Pop artists. Johns' works included paintings of target symbols similar to those used for archery. Some artists with more experience in commercial art were inspired by Neo-Dada ideas and Happenings. These artists, such as Andy Warhol, Roy Lichtenstein, and Claes Oldenburg, tried including popular subjects in their work. They formed the core of the Pop Art movement.

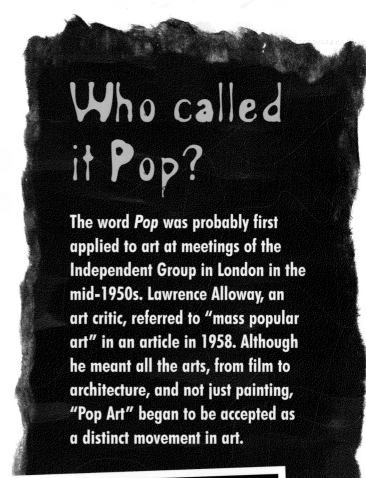

Who called it Pop?

The word *Pop* was probably first applied to art at meetings of the Independent Group in London in the mid-1950s. Lawrence Alloway, an art critic, referred to "mass popular art" in an article in 1958. Although he meant all the arts, from film to architecture, and not just painting, "Pop Art" began to be accepted as a distinct movement in art.

Andy Warhol (1928–87) was known as the "Prince of Pop," because of his great influence on the Pop Art movement and on 1960s culture.

James Rosenquist's *President Elect* (1960) is a mixed advertisement for President John F. Kennedy, a slice of chocolate cake, and a car. The message of the painting was that politicians are manufactured to appeal to the masses, just like the other products.

New realists

U.S. Pop Art came of age in October 1962, through an exhibition at the Sidney Janis Gallery in New York. Janis had a reputation for showing the best in contemporary art. In the 1962 exhibition called *The New Realists*, he showed paintings and collages by European artists, such as Christo, from Bulgaria and Yves Klein from France, but he gave much more wall space to works by Warhol, Oldenburg, Tom Wesselmann, Jim Dine, and other younger American Pop artists. The European artists were already highly regarded and people wanted to buy their art. Through being associated with them at the exhibition, U.S. Pop Art became important and collectable, too.

U.S. versus British Pop

In general, British artists were most interested in putting popular images together in a new context, for example, in collages. In the United States, Pop artists often made copies of images that they overlaid, arranged, or transformed. This was their way of making a comment about American society. For example, Warhol made prints of the electric chair, which was designed legally to kill criminals. He said: *"When you see a gruesome image again and again, it does not really have an effect."* By reproducing the chair, he wanted people to think about how we can get used to looking at even the most violent images without being affected emotionally.

Everything is Beautiful

Andy Warhol once said that *"Everything is beautiful. Pop is everything."* He meant that anything could be transformed into art that people would want to look at. Although all Pop artists developed their own styles and favorite subjects, they shared broad themes and ideas in their art.

New icons

The word **icon** is often used to mean an image that has sacred or cultural significance for people. Icons of the Virgin Mary, Jesus Christ, and the Crucifixion, for example, are important to Christians, especially in the Orthodox Church, and have been made by artists since the Middle Ages. Pop artists created new icons for the modern age, choosing their subjects from the media: famous movie actresses, such as Marilyn Monroe and Joan Crawford, singers such as Elvis Presley, and well-known comic and cartoon characters, including the detective Dick Tracy and Walt Disney's Mickey Mouse.

Pop artists realized that people were also affected deeply by photographs of significant world events, in newspapers, magazines, and movie newsreels. In the 1960s, as Pop Art developed, there was growing anxiety in the United States about the **Cold War** with Russia and the threat of nuclear war.

The Only Blonde in the World (1963), by British artist Pauline Boty, is one of many Pop tributes to the movie icon Marilyn Monroe, who died in 1962.

Artists such as James Rosenquist used the mushroom cloud that forms after a nuclear explosion as an icon symbolizing horrific war.

From ordinary to extraordinary

Pop artists believed that images of the most ordinary objects or places could be icons. Examples range from prints of Campbell's soup cans and Coke bottles, to models of cakes and detergent boxes. Warhol liked the fact that products such as these were familiar and bought by anyone, from rich to poor. Pop artists, such as Ed Ruscha, made paintings of road signs and gas stations. Others, such as Robert Indiana, painted large colored canvases of words such as "Love" or "Eat," and numbers that look as if they might have been stolen off of massive billboards.

Robert Indiana's *Love* icon was first used for a Christmas card design, but has since become a sculpture in 20 locations worldwide.

The art of Marilyn

When Marilyn Monroe died suddenly in 1962, stories and articles about her filled the media. Some focused on her acting talent, and others on whether the glare of constant publicity had led to her death. Pop artists, including Andy Warhol and Pauline Boty, created endless variations on Marilyn images. In 1967, there was a tribute exhibition at the Sidney Janis Gallery showing just the art of Marilyn.

Try it yourself

Love and other big words
Robert Indiana chose "Love" as an icon, because the word had religious and political significance in the 1960s. At this time, young people became increasingly antiwar and the slogan "Make love not war" was popular. Choose a word that you think has meaning, then choose a font style and design a Pop icon.

Multiple art

In the art world, people had usually thought that the rarer a work, the greater its quality. It was also assumed that a work only had worth if it was made by the artist's own hand. Some Pop artists, including Warhol, had other ideas. They believed that identical or similar copies of an original work were equal in worth to the original, even if they were mass-produced like objects made in factories. The artists called these repeat artworks **multiples**. Either an unlimited quantity, or more commonly, a limited number or **edition** of multiples was made. Some of the most famous multiples include Warhol's prints of Mao Zedong, the Chinese leader in the 1960s, dollar bills, and soup cans.

Pop artists made multiples partly to experiment with variations in color or style on a single theme. Jasper Johns said: *"Take an object, do something with it, and then do something else with it."* The artists also hoped that making multiples would make their new art accessible to the general public. Rapidly produced copies were more affordable for people to buy and show in their homes.

Popularizing Pop

Some art critics and viewers in the 1960s thought that Pop Art was simply copies of ads and a disappointing new direction in art. A respected American art critic, Hilton Kramer, said: *"Pop Art does not tell us what it feels like to be living through the present moment of civilization. Its social effect is simply to reconcile us to a world of commodities [things to buy], banalities [uninteresting and predictable subjects], and vulgarities."*

On the other hand, many people did appreciate Pop Art, not least because it was widely seen in all types of media, from magazines to movies. For example, a TV movie in 1962 called *Pop Goes the Easel*, by director Ken Russell, showed the work of British Pop artists Peter Blake and Derek Boshier to a wide audience. Pop Art also appeared on the covers of records by 1960s bands, such as The Who and The Beatles. And Pop Art styles influenced new fashions for young people, seen on London's famous Carnaby Street.

Pop banners

During a newspaper strike in New York from December 1962 to April 1963, there could be little press publicity for city art galleries. Robert Graham organized Pop artists to design banners that he could hang outside his gallery to advertise upcoming shows. People liked the designs so much that when the strike was over, Graham and associates formed the Betsy Ross Flag and Banner Company. The company chose 45 of the banner designs and made a limited edition of 20 of each one, for people to buy. The banners popularized the idea of the multiple and made Americans reassess their ideas about originality in art.

The cover for the Beatles' album *Sergeant Pepper's Lonely Hearts Club Band* was designed by Pop artist Peter Blake. The image on the front featured a collage of over 50 celebrities, ranging from sportspeople and spiritual leaders, to movie stars and poets.

Pop Pictures

Pop Art comes in many forms, from painted canvases to plaster models. However, most Pop artists created pieces to be shown on the wall, in galleries or homes. They painted, printed, and made movies of their images.

Painting styles

In general, the Pop style in paint or print was **impersonal**. Pop artists were not trying to express their feelings when they painted, as the Abstract Expressionists had done. Therefore, most Pop Art has no **gestural marks**, such as thickly applied paint and obvious brushstrokes, which are a record of the artist at work. Instead, Pop artists wanted the way they worked to be like an industrial process. They used oil or acrylic paints, developed by companies after World War II, to paint on canvas. Some painted with enamel paints on steel.

Artists such as Warhol and Lichtenstein painted areas of flat color with smooth brushstrokes. They used bright, even tones with little shading, to make even **three-dimensional** subjects look **two-dimensional**. Others built up thicker layers of paint, known as **impasto**. Wayne Thiebaud used impasto to make thick icing on the cakes in his *Cake Counter* look more realistic.

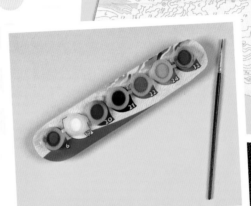

A paint-by-number kit helps beginners to paint detailed designs in lots of colors.

Paint-by-number

After World War II, there was generally more leisure time than before. Some paint manufacturers tried to encourage people to paint as a hobby, by selling paint-by-number kits. A kit consisted of a board or canvas with the outline of a picture on it, divided into little numbered sections, and numbered pots of paints. The amateur painter just needed to use paint number 2 on all sections of the picture numbered 2, and so on, to complete the whole painting.

Andy Warhol made a Pop icon of these types of paintings in *Do It Yourself, Seascape* (1962). This flatly painted, brightly colored picture of a house, with boats and the sea in the background, has small numbers painted on top of each color.

Patrick Caulfield's *Coloured Still Life* (1967) is typical of his distinctive Pop style.

Pop technology

Pop artists used technology to help them paint images that looked realistic. Warhol transferred photographs from newspapers onto transparent glass or plastic plates to make slides. Then he used a projector to shine light through a slide and through a magnifying lens, so that an enlarged image appeared on a canvas hung on the wall. He painted this projected image.

Painters, such as Peter Phillips and James Rosenquist, used **airbrushes** to create photographlike paintings.

In a line

Some artists developed their own characteristic styles. Patrick Caulfield, a British Pop artist, often painted simple interiors containing a few objects, from chairs to fruit. He reduced the objects to easily recognizable icons by painting heavy black outlines around their single-color shapes, a little like the outlines around some cartoon characters.

Airbrushes are spray guns that use compressed air to blow very thin coats of paint onto a surface. They allow artists to create subtle gradations of color and tone.

Paint comes out here

Direction of air

Pop printing

Pop artists liked to print images to create multiples and even single pieces, because printing is an indirect, often mechanical process. Printing involves transferring an original design or image from one medium to another. There are many ways of creating an original design for printing, such as scratching the design on metal plates or drawing it with waxy crayon on stone blocks. However, the favorite Pop print technique was **screen-printing**. Before the 1960s, this was largely a commercial process, used to print images on posters and T-shirts. Pop artists used it to create icons.

How screen printing works

The artist makes a screen by stretching a fabric mesh over a wooden frame. A design is made on the screen by "blocking" some areas of it. This blocking may be done by applying special paints. A flexible rubber strip called a **squeegee** is then dragged across the screen, forcing ink or paint through the unblocked areas onto some paper or canvas.

The process is sometimes called silkscreen, because, originally, a fine mesh of silk strands was used, as for making silk stockings. But Pop artists often used nylon and other man-made fabrics.

Warhol typically used a photographic technique for blocking his designs. He covered the screen with a light-sensitive fluid and projected a slide onto it. The fluid hardened and blocked the screen in the light parts of the photo, but not in the dark parts. Warhol used this technique to screen-print canvases with images of famous people's faces, banknotes, and soup cans.

Different layers

A screen-print is typically made in several stages, with a different element or color being added to the image each time. For example, a first screen might be a black and white photograph of a face. Then different screens are used to add the color of skin and hair. The blocked part of each screen is a different shape.

Warhol's Factory

Warhol once said: *"It would be terrific if everyone was alike."* He believed that it was desirable for artists to be "boring" and not really involved at all stages in production of their art. In the early 1960s, Warhol did his printing himself. He would then sell a soup can print for $100. From 1963 onward, he was famous enough to employ many assistants in a large studio he called The Factory. Warhol chose the images, and the assistants prepared the screens and mass-produced prints on anything from canvases to hang on the wall, to shopping bags and other objects. Sometimes they even signed the objects on his behalf! By 1964, a large Warhol soup can print would cost $1,500. Today, his Factory prints sell for tens of thousands of dollars.

Warhol made the images in his multiples slightly different from each other. For example, his series of 32 prints of cans of Campbell's soup looked identical at first glance, but closer examination showed that they were labeled as different flavors. In other series, the differences were not so great. Prints of the Chinese Communist party leader Mao Zedong, for instance, all used the same portrait. Each was made unique by adding coarse brushstrokes of different-colored paint around the image of Mao's face.

This painting of Mao Zedong by Richard Pettibone is almost a direct copy of Andy Warhol prints from the 1960s. Warhol usually repeated the subjects he used in his multiples or series of prints, but made each slightly different from the rest.

Try it yourself

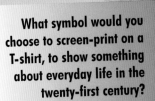

Screen-print a Pop Art T-shirt

What you will need:

A plain T-shirt

An embroidery hoop 8 inches (20 centimeters) wide

Craft glue

An old pair of pantyhose

A chisel-edged paintbrush with stiff bristles, about 1/2 inch (10 millimeters) wide

Fabric paints

1 Find a simple image of a common sign or symbol to use on your T-shirt. You can use an Internet search engine or look in magazines, books, newspapers, and catalogs and scan in what you find. Some suggestions are shown on this page.

2 Now enlarge your image so that it fits inside a circle with a diameter of 8 inches (20 centimeters). You can do this by copying and pasting the image into a graphics software package, such as Paint, or by using a photocopier.

3 Print the image in a circle, in black, on white paper.

> **What symbol would you choose to screen-print on a T-shirt, to show something about everyday life in the twenty-first century?**

4 Cut a square of fabric from the pantyhose, larger than your embroidery hoop. Unscrew the hoops, stretch the fabric over the large hoop, and use the smaller hoop to trap the fabric.

5 Place the hoop on top of your design. Use a pencil or pen to draw around the design you can see through the fabric.

6 Turn the hoop over and neatly paint glue over the areas of your design that you do not want paint to go through (right).

7 Wash the brush and let the glue on the fabric dry. Now you are ready to print.

8 Put a piece of card inside the T-shirt and place the hoop on top. Hold it firmly, and use the brush to dab a generous amount of fabric paint through the unblocked parts of your design onto the T-shirt.

9 Carefully lift up the hoop and let the paint dry. You may need to ask an adult to iron the paint onto the T-shirt to make it stick.

10 If you like the design on the screen, why not ask an adult if you can print it on other fabric objects, such as plain towels or aprons, or make posters, perhaps using other colors?

Dot painting

Roy Lichtenstein is famous for making paintings that look like printed drawings, enlarged. Like other Pop artists, he worked mostly from a particular category of images. Whereas Warhol represented products seen for sale in supermarkets, Lichtenstein took his subjects from comics, mostly because these had fascinated him since he was a child. Generally, he chose images from war comics, showing firing machine guns or explosions, or from romantic comics, showing women looking sad or worried.

Lichtenstein always worked in the same way. He enlarged and projected a slide of a cartoon onto a large canvas and used the projected picture as a guide for his painting. Usually he slightly changed the image to make it his own. Lichtenstein painted the **Benday dots**, which are visible on enlarged comics, with the aid of thin metal stencils called Benday screens. He carefully painted through the regularly spaced holes of the Benday screen onto his canvas.

Benday dots

The comics from which Lichtenstein took his subjects were printed using the Benday dot printing process. Evenly spaced dots of black, yellow, magenta (red), and cyan (blue) were used to create different tones and colors. For example, yellow dots overlapped by cyan dots made green. The dots were also of different sizes. Fine dots produced a lighter tone than large dots, because there was more unprinted space between them.

This printing process was named after a printer and illustrator called Benjamin Day (1810–89).

You can see how the paler gray areas of this hand are made by smaller black dots, and the darkest areas are made by large black dots. The dots are evenly spaced, but appear farther apart when they are smaller in size.

In color printing, all colors and tones can be made from cyan, magenta, yellow, and black.

Warhol was both director and cameraman on some movies he made in The Factory in the mid-1960s. Many of his movies show very ordinary things happening, but they became famous mostly because Warhol made them.

Pop film

Some Pop artists also created art using the medium of film. They realized that portable movie cameras could easily and quickly record day-to-day activities, which could then be shown in galleries. Warhol made over 60 movies during the mid-1960s, in his Factory (see page 20). Some are like very slow-moving paintings. For example, *Sleep* is a movie of one of Warhol's friends sleeping for 6 hours, and another called *Eat* shows a man eating a mushroom for 45 minutes! *Chelsea Girls* consisted of two separate movies, projected side-by-side onto the screen. The viewer's attention shifted from one movie to the other when the sound for each was turned up or down.

Richard Lester is a movie director known as the father of the music video. He made movies called *Help!* and *A Hard Day's Night*, featuring The Beatles. In *Help!*, he showed the musicians not only seriously playing their latest music, but also fooling around while it was playing in the background and taking part in an adventure story. In so doing, he helped make The Beatles famous even to people not interested in their music. Today, it is common for music groups and singers to make videos, from footage of them performing in strange settings to animation based on the songs' words.

3D Pop Art

Some Pop artists constructed their art in three dimensions—with height, depth, and breadth. Some built out from flat paintings or made iconic sculptures out of unusual materials. Others filled gallery spaces with sculptures and real objects, to create interactive, walk-in art.

Adding depth

Pop artists sometimes used mixed materials to help bring their art off the wall. Jasper Johns made his first flag image by painting on a real U.S. flag. First, he stuck the flag on a piece of wood. Then he stuck clippings from newspapers on top of the flag, and over the clippings he painted white stars on blue, and red and white stripes. The paint he used was encaustic, which is a mixture of color pigment and hot, melted wax. Encaustic can only be worked for a short time before it sets hard, forming an opaque, textured layer. In Johns' work, only parts of the newspaper clippings show through the encaustic. By building up layers, Johns added physical depth to the work.

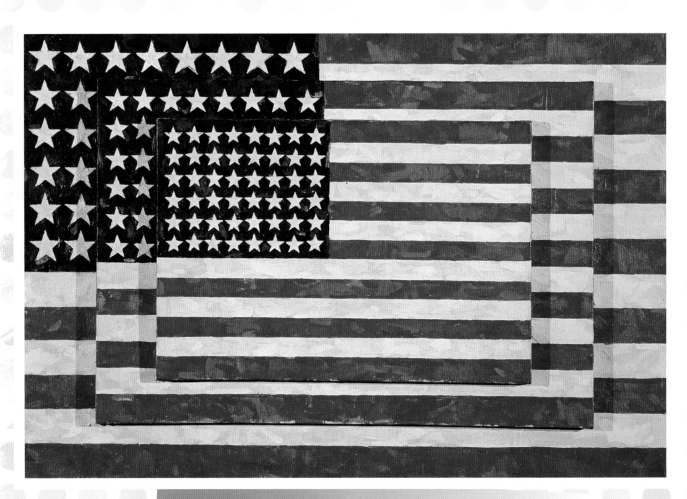

Jasper Johns' *Three Flags* (1958) is painted on three canvases of diminishing sizes, stacked together. Johns added depth for this work by building outward. It helped to transform the usually flat flag image into a three-dimensional object.

Variations on a theme

Jasper Johns said that the idea of painting the "Stars and Stripes" came to him in a dream in 1954. He was attracted to the different meanings of the flag to people in the United States. For example, the flag is a symbol of nationality, but also of involvement in wars. So he painted many versions, such as green stripes on orange, white stars and stripes on a white background, with too many stars, and superimposed flags of different sizes. When he had exhausted that idea, Johns went on to paint variations on other themes, including 25 different target paintings and many with the names of colors painted on different-colored backgrounds.

Monogram (1955–59) is one of Rauschenberg's most famous sculptures. It combines a part-painted goat with a tire around its middle and a painted canvas!

Unusual media

In the 1950s, Robert Rauschenberg created a series of very unusual 3D paintings that had a big influence on Pop. He called the paintings "combines," because each combined painting on canvas with found objects, also fully or partially painted. The objects included pieces of magazines, leather, canvas and other fabrics, metal, electric cable, and even whole items, from stuffed animals, bird wings, or skulls to car tires, chairs, and street signs. In many of the paintings, the objects are separate from the canvas, but connected to it with pieces of wood, string, or cable. Rauschenberg believed that *"A picture is more like the real world when it's made out of the real world."* Unlike later Pop artists, he chose real, discarded objects in his images and did not use them as symbols of current culture.

Realistic sculptures

A few Pop artists used traditional sculpture materials, such as plaster of Paris and the metal **bronze**, to create realistic models of their subjects. Jasper Johns made bronze **casts** of real objects, including a pot of used paintbrushes and beer cans.

George Segal was a Pop sculptor who used life-sized casts of real people for his works. To make the casts, he draped bandages soaked in wet plaster around the bodies of his models. He cut off the bandages when they had dried hard. Segal never painted the casts, leaving them in white plaster. He always exhibited his people in realistic settings. For example, an early work shows a woman washing one of her feet in a real sink. Another shows a man walking past the window of a restaurant, where a single, possibly lonely, woman is sitting at a table.

The soft approach

A sculpture is a 3D artwork, traditionally made from hard materials so that it can stand on its own and show its form. But Claes Oldenburg, the most famous Pop sculptor, is best known for using very soft materials.

From these, he created giant versions of familiar hard items found in the home, such as telephones, typewriters, light switches, and sinks. To make a sculpture, Oldenburg cut out pieces of vinyl or canvas, sewed them into the basic forms of the object he was creating, and filled these with enough soft stuffing to make the shapes recognizable. For example, a drum kit is made of several cylinders of different sizes. He displayed his finished sculptures on metal frames so that they drooped.

This sculpture by George Segal, entitled *Patrons*, is typical of his life-sized, realistic plaster figures in sparse settings.

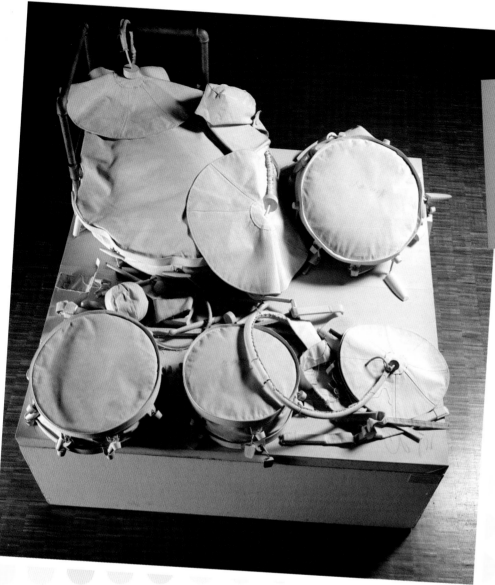

"Ghost" Drum Set (1972) by Claes Oldenburg shows how using unexpected materials and scales for his soft sculptures transformed popular objects. His "ghost" series of sculptures were all-white versions of earlier colorful vinyl works.

Increasing the size of everyday objects and making them from a different material transformed them into something unlikely. A soft drum kit could not be played and a droopy washstand could not hold water. Oldenburg was getting people to look at the world around them in a new way.

Try it yourself

Make a Pop Art Popsicle sculpture

In the 1960s, Oldenburg made enormous fabric items of food, including a hamburger, hotdog, and ice-cream cone. You could use an old pillowcase to make a soft sculpture of a frozen Popsicle. Stuff the pillowcase with crumpled newspaper, and find a piece of wood the right length and width to look like the Popsicle stick. Stitch, tape, or staple the open end of the pillowcase to hold in the stuffing and stick. You could decorate the Popsicle with scraps of fabric to make it look realistic, or even sew the pillowcase to make it look as though a bite has been taken out of the Popsicle.

Oldenburg's *The Store* was a store with a difference. It was an artwork made to sell parts of itself, with the artist's help.

Installations

An **installation** is a work of art that includes the space it occupies, such as a whole room. It is usually made up of several different elements. Some Pop artists made installations as realistic settings for their sculptures. In 1961, Oldenburg transformed his small studio in New York into an installation called *The Store*. In it, on store shelves, he displayed real objects including stockings and dresses, alongside sculptures that he had made rapidly and roughly by sticking plaster-soaked bandages over chicken wire. These sculptures were of objects including sandwiches, cans of soda, plates of meat, a cash register, and a mirror. Most were daubed with shiny metallic paint.

Store prices then and now

One hundred items were for sale in *The Store*, and Oldenburg priced each one. He sold a pie crust for $324.98, but most of the objects were much cheaper than that. The objects were not particularly valued as art and got damaged over time, so they are quite rare today. In 1989, a "Bacon and Egg" plaster sculpture sold at an auction for $495,000!

Everything in *The Store* was for sale. Oldenburg printed business cards, stationery, and posters to advertise it, and distributed them in galleries and other places to entice "shoppers." He even stood at the cash register and gave receipts when people bought his work.

The American Supermarket

In 1964, several well-known Pop artists got together for an exhibition at the Bianchini Gallery called *The American Supermarket*. At this installation, multiples were for sale. Warhol made stacks of detergent boxes. Robert Watts made wax tomatoes and printed false dollar bills. Oldenburg cast baked potatoes out of plastic, and Lichtenstein made clay dishes. Warhol and Lichtenstein printed shopping bags with images in Benday dots of soup cans and cooked turkey, which sold for $2 and $12 respectively. Some of the objects were for practical use. For example, people could eat off the dishes and carry the bags for shopping around town.

Try it yourself

Install your own food store
You can easily use air-drying clay to make hamburger, sausage, fruit, and other food shapes, and paint them in suitable colors.

You could also try making larger shapes out of crumpled chicken wire, taping newspaper over, and painting them. (Take care not to scratch your hands on the sharp ends of the wire.) Then make some shelves to display your goods and make a price list.

The Influence of Pop Art

From the second half of the 1960s onward, gallery owners had a wider range of art styles to sell than just Pop. However, the Pop approach to art did not die. It spread internationally and forward into the present, constantly changing as different people, events, and objects became familiar to the public. Today, public interest in Pop Art is as high as ever, because the consumer lifestyle continues to spread.

Op Art

Optical or **Op Art** was widely seen as Pop's successor in 1965–66. The aim of Op artists was to create optical illusions for the viewer and therefore, intense reactions to their work. Artists such as Victor Vasarely, based in Paris, and Bridget Riley, based in London, used lines, shapes, and colors to give the effect of motion. Many people liked Op because it was abstract and did not rely on symbols like Pop. However, the Pop idea that anything could be art had a big effect on how people accepted this new art movement.

What happened to the Pop pioneers?

Several of the original Pop artists continued to work on popular subjects, but in a different way from in the late 1960s. For example, Warhol made prints of new subjects, including skulls, guns, the composer Beethoven, and artists including himself, up to his death in 1987. Roy Lichtenstein made large Pop sculptures, sometimes of details from his earlier paintings, for public spaces. From the late 1970s onward, Claes Oldenburg made colossal sculptures of small objects, such as hand tools, sports equipment, and food, with the help of a professional metalwork factory. For example, *Saw, Sawing* (1996) is a saw made of steel, plastic, and foam, that measures 50 feet (15.4 meters) high. It is displayed in a public square in Tokyo, Japan.

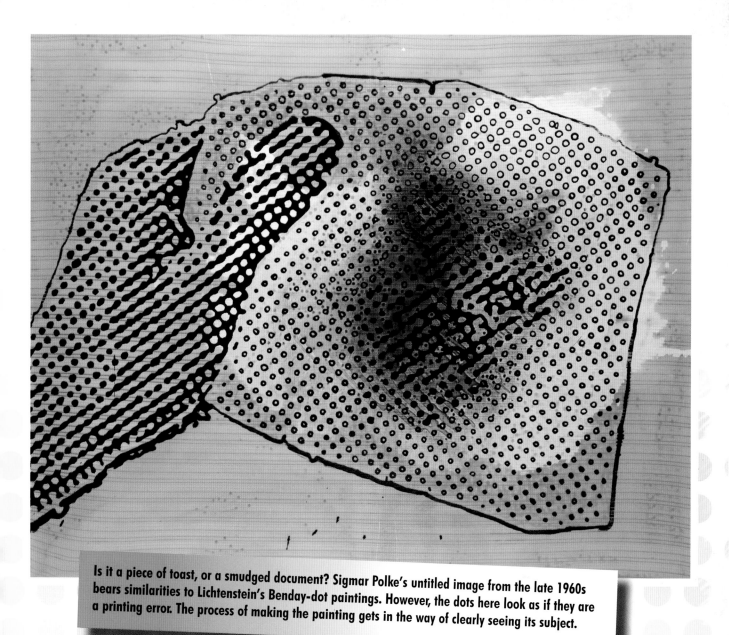

Is it a piece of toast, or a smudged document? Sigmar Polke's untitled image from the late 1960s bears similarities to Lichtenstein's Benday-dot paintings. However, the dots here look as if they are a printing error. The process of making the painting gets in the way of clearly seeing its subject.

Newer realism

The influence of Pop Art spread from the United States worldwide. In Spain, artists such as Eduardo Arroyo focused on the importance of icons in Pop Art, painting brightly colored pictures of bullfighters and political leaders, for example. In Dusseldorf, Germany, artists including Gerhard Richter and Sigmar Polke were more interested in the realism of Pop Art. They described this German Pop as **Capitalist Realism**. Richter painted copies of images projected from his own photos, then used sponges and squeegees to smear the paint and blur the images.

Polke painted dot pictures something like Lichtenstein's. They looked like details of blurred or imperfect prints.

In the late 1960s and early 1970s, in the United States, some artists tried to make their images completely identical to the subjects they were based on. Richard Estes used an airbrush to paint giant, exact copies of photographs of normal subjects, such as caravans. Duane Hanson made lifelike sculptures of subjects such as American tourists. This work was usually called **Photorealism**.

Experimenting with photography

Several artists were fascinated by the Polaroid instant camera, which first became available in the mid-1960s. Conventional cameras of that time used film, which took from hours to days to be developed into photographs and printed. But the Polaroid instant camera produced its own prints of photos, straight after each one was taken. The inks on Polaroid prints took a few minutes to dry, and this was used by Lucas Samaras to make a series of photo-transformations in the early 1970s. He took Polaroid photos of himself and smeared the ink before it dried, to create distorted expressions and body forms.

David Hockney, a British artist, produced some art that was Pop, such as a painting that includes a large tea box. He is best known for paintings in the 1970s of water splashes in swimming pools and celebrity friends, and also for his "joiners." This was Hockney's word for images made of many overlapping photos of a subject or scene, taken from different viewpoints and at different times. (Another word for this is a **photomontage**.) Some joiners created a more 3D view of a scene, such as a desert landscape, than a single photo of it. Others showed a progression of events, such as a group of friends talking and reacting to each other.

Try it yourself

Make a photomontage self-portrait

Ask a friend to take about 20 photographs of your face from slightly different viewpoints, using a digital camera. Print the results as small photos. Then arrange and rearrange them, overlapping, on a large piece of paper, to create a single image that you think best represents you. Carefully stick the prints down or even take another single photo of the "joiner."

Gilbert and George

Two of the most unusual artists since Pop are Gilbert and George. From the late 1960s, these two British artists decided to call themselves "living sculptures." They usually dress in matching suits, walk in step, and spend all their time together. Their most typical pieces are enormous photomontages featuring themselves and other subjects, and usually representing controversial issues of the time, including law-breaking teenagers, racism, and terrorism. They have said: *"We want our art to speak across the barriers of knowledge directly to People about their Life and not about their knowledge of art. The twentieth century has been cursed with an art that cannot be understood."*

Street (1983) is typical of Gilbert and George's style. It features the two artists as icons shouting in front of busy streets. Do you think their shouts are a conversation or a protest against city traffic?

STREET

Art for everyone

Pop artists made almost any object acceptable as a work of art, and in virtually any setting. Murals on buildings, pictures drawn in chalk on the sidewalk, and even some graffiti on walls are seen as **street art**. However, painting or writing graffiti is also considered to be a type of vandalism and is illegal.

Some street artists have become quite famous as a result of their Pop subjects. The American street artist, Keith Haring, found fame after making chalk drawings of iconic images, such as babies, dogs, and angels, on unused black advertising panels in a New York subway station between 1980 and 1985. Sometimes he completed up to 40 drawings a day.

The British self-styled "art terrorist," Banksy, started out in the late 1980s by spraying humorous graffiti on walls, using stencils as painting guides. He now paints and prints collectable works, some in the style of Andy Warhol or adaptations of famous paintings from longer ago, such as the *Mona Lisa*.

Banksy also carries out acts to publicize his views on contemporary culture and celebrity. In 2006, he wanted to convey the idea that some people become famous simply because they are rich and famous. He removed 500 copies of Paris Hilton's debut CD from music shops and replaced them with copies of his own disc, which had song titles such as "What Have I Done?" and "Why Am I Famous?"

The continued appeal of Pop Art

Some artists continue to make Pop Art out of familiar subjects today. Their work is often called New Pop or Neo-Pop. American artist Jeff Koons makes sculptures out of unexpected media, such as an enormous balloon dog and a shiny metal eggshell. The British artist, Damien Hirst, first became famous after exhibiting preserved sharks and sawn-up sheep and cows in tanks, but he works in other media, too. In 2007, he exhibited a skull cast from platinum metal and encrusted with over 8,000 diamonds.

The work of the original Pop artists, including Warhol and Lichtenstein, remains very popular. Many of their messages about art, culture, mass production, and icons apply just as much to modern-day life as they did in the 1950s and 1960s.

Puppy (1992) is a 40-foot (12-meter) tall metal sculpture by Jeff Koons, designed to hold flower pots. It changes as the flowers grow and then bloom through the seasons. This Neo-Pop piece is by the Guggenheim Museum in Bilbao, Spain.

Japanese Pop Art factory

Takashi Murakami runs a studio called Kaikai Kiki in Tokyo. He designs contemporary Pop Art objects and supervises his assistants to make them, a little like at Warhol's Factory. The objects produced include prints, one-of-a-kind sculptures, and mass-produced toys and candies. Murakami uses recurring favorite subjects, such as a mouselike character called Mr. DOB and colorful mushrooms, and a graphic style popular in Japanese comics and cartoons.

Getting into Art

Has reading about Pop Art inspired you to become an artist yourself? Do you find yourself doodling new images all the time, or fascinated by the way Pop sculptors fashioned those giant fabric hamburgers? If so, perhaps you are a popular artist of the future!

Practice makes perfect

If you want to be an artist, practice does make perfect. That may sound like a boring cliché, but it is true. So you need to get yourself a sketchbook and develop your skills. Draw different kinds of objects, from cans of beans to fall leaves in a woodland. Remember Jasper Johns' comment: *"Take an object, do something with it, and then do something else with it."* Why not pick an object and then try drawing it in different media, from pencils to oil paints? Also try using new techniques, such as printing, to create different images of the object.

Experiment with the computer and programs such as Photoshop, manipulating photographs or images that you have drawn to create bold, new Pop Art-style images. Many Pop artists would have done so if they had the chance, as Andy Warhol said: *"Paintings are too hard. The things I want to show are mechanical. Machines have less problems. I'd like to be a machine, wouldn't you?"*

Nowadays, you can use a computer program to adapt images and make many different versions of them. Texting is a subject that Pop artists might have used for their images, if cell phones had existed in their day.

Art classes

At school, you may be able to attend extra art classes at lunchtime or after school, or the art teacher may let you use the art facilities in your spare time. In many towns, art classes are also held in local galleries or colleges. When you finish high school you may decide to study art, or graphic art, at college. At college, you will have access to large studios, print workshops, darkrooms, and many other facilities that can help you to grow as an artist. When you apply for a place at an art school or a university, it is useful to have a portfolio of your work. A portfolio is a collection of your best pieces of work, those that show your skills and interests. You could even include some of the art you created when doing the "Try it yourself" activities in this book.

Visiting art exhibitions

Visiting exhibitions is a great experience for anyone, but especially for a budding artist. When you visit a gallery, think about the composition of the art you see, the medium and colors used, and the subjects covered. How could these things inspire your own work?

Many museums and art galleries around the world have examples of Pop Art.

Keep a record!

If you want to be an artist, you need to be thinking about images all the time. Try to keep a folder or scrapbook of images from magazines and books, or pictures by other artists that you find interesting. It is also a good idea to carry a camera with you, so that you can photograph anything interesting you see, or anything everyday and ordinary that you see in a new light and might want to draw or make an image of one day.

Lives of the Artists

Peter Blake (born 1932)

British Pop Art pioneer Peter Blake is perhaps most famous for his cover design for The Beatles' album *Sergeant Pepper's Lonely Hearts Club Band* (1967). After studying at the Royal Academy of Art in London and traveling the world, he featured in the Pop Art movie, *Pop Goes the Easel*, in 1962, and the following year had his first solo exhibition. His images are inspired by popular culture, such as ads, and produced using techniques such as collage, drawing, and painting.

Patrick Caulfield (1936–2005)

An English painter and printmaker, Patrick Caulfield became associated with Pop Art after his pictures were in the New Generation exhibition at the Whitechapel Art Gallery, London, in 1964. His paintings simplify objects to a basic black outline in order to present ordinary images as mysterious. His major works include *Still-life with Dagger* (1963), *Portrait of Juan Gris* (1963), and *Greece Expiring on the Ruins of Missolongh* (1963).

Jasper Johns (born 1930)

The U.S. artist, Jasper Johns, knew he wanted to be an artist from the age of five. In 1953, at 23 years old, he moved to New York where he became friends with the artist Robert Rauschenberg. He liked to "draw things the mind already knows" and is famous for his paintings of flags, such as *White Flag* (1955). His other major works include *False Start* (1959) and *Study for Skin* (1962).

Richard Hamilton (born 1922)

Richard Hamilton was a key figure in the British Pop Art movement. He studied at St. Martin's School of Art and later at the Royal Academy in London, and worked as an assistant to the Dada artist, Marcel Duchamp. He cofounded the Independent Group at the Institute of Contemporary Arts (ICA) in London. Key works include *Just What Is It That Makes Today's Homes So Different, So Appealing?* (1955) and *Hommage à Chrysler Corp.* (1957).

Roy Lichtenstein (1923–97)

In the 1950s, the American artist, Roy Lichtenstein, met artists such as Jim Dine and Claes Oldenburg, who were experimenting with different kinds of art based on everyday life. Then, from 1961, he began to make paintings of comic-strip figures, using his Benday dots, lettering, and speech or thought bubbles. By the mid-1960s, he was also making Pop Art versions of paintings by famous artists such as Cézanne. Lichtenstein's major works include *The Kiss* (1961) and *Whaam!* (1963).

Robert Rauschenberg (1925–2008)

Robert Rauschenberg became interested in art after a chance visit to a gallery while serving as a nurse in a U.S. naval hospital during World War II. Later, when he was an art student, one of his projects involved going out and finding objects that could be described as interesting. His "combined paintings" used photographs, "found" objects such as coke bottles, and stuffed animals, partially covered with paint. They include *Monogram* (1955–59) and *Express* (1963).

Claes Oldenburg (born 1929)

Claes Oldenburg was born in Sweden, but spent most of his life in the United States, initially working as a comic-strip artist. In 1956, he moved to New York City, where he soon became a prominent figure in Happenings. In 1959, he exhibited a series of images, made from a mix of drawings, collages, and papier-mâché, and in 1961, he opened *The Store* in his studio. His famous works include *Soft Bathtub* (1966) and the giant outdoor sculpture, *Lipstick (Ascending) on Caterpillar Tracks* (1974).

Andy Warhol (1928–87)

Andy Warhol began his career as a commercial artist, and was so successful that he won prizes for some of his advertisements for shoes. In 1962, he made a painting of Campbell's soup cans. Throughout the 1960s, he printed multiple images of anything from coke bottles and soup cans to Marilyn Monroe and Muhammad Ali. He employed other artists in his studio, called The Factory, to make a lot of his later art, and also made over 300 avant-garde (new and experimental) movies.

Tom Wesselmann (1931–2004)

An American painter, sculptor, and printmaker, Tom Wesselman originally planned to become a cartoonist. He became known as a founder of American Pop Art, due to works such as his giant still lifes. These were made up from common household objects and collage elements taken from popular advertising images. One example is *Still Life #20* (1962).

Pop Art Timeline

1914–18 World War I leads to massive destruction in Europe and causes people to question the old rules of society.

1924 Surrealism begins. Surrealist artists were interested in using images from popular culture, especially cinema, and also from dreams.

1937 The Surrealist Salvador Dalí includes popular actress Shirley Temple in a painting.

1939–45 World War II rages in Europe and also spreads into Africa and Asia. The conflict kills millions, but the U.S. economy is revitalized by manufacturing for the war.

1951 The Festival of Britain celebrates British design and symbolizes the recovery of Britain after World War II.

1953 The Independent Group starts to meet at the Institute of Contemporary Arts, London.

1954 Jasper Johns creates his first Flag painting.

1956 Elvis Presley has his first number one hit.

1956 (cont.) The first British Pop Art is made by Richard Hamilton and other Independent Group artists contributing to the *This is Tomorrow* exhibition in London. Images used include Marilyn Monroe and comics.

1957 Universal Limited Art Editions company is established in New York as a center of print technology and excellence. It teaches techniques that become important in the work of Pop artists such as Andy Warhol.

1958 Jasper Johns and Robert Rauschenberg have their first solo exhibitions at the Leo Castelli Gallery, New York.

1959 The first Happenings are organized in New York by Allan Kaprow.

1960 Andy Warhol does his first paintings based on cartoons of Dick Tracy, Superman, and Popeye.

1961 Claes Oldenburg opens *The Store*, a studio made to look like a shop, where he shows objects in painted plaster and stages Happenings.

1962 Roy Lichtenstein shows his first works based on comic-strip frames, painted in Benday dots, at the Leo Castelli Gallery.

Warhol creates a painting of Campbell's soup cans.

The New Realists exhibition at the Sidney Janis Gallery in New York shows work by European New Realist artists alongside that of Pop artists.

Marilyn Monroe dies.

1962/63 Ken Russell's TV movie *Pop goes the Easel* features the British artists Peter Blake and Derek Boshier.

1963 Warhol transforms a loft in New York into a studio he calls The Factory.

U.S. President John F. Kennedy is assassinated in Dallas, Texas.

The Capitalist Realism art movement starts in Germany.

1964 The Grand Jury Prize at the 34th Venice Biennale, the biggest art prize of its time, is awarded to Rauschenberg.

Paintings that create optical effects for the viewer are first named Op Art.

1964 (cont.) Federal voting rights legislation passed by U.S. Congress.

1965 Large numbers of U.S. troops are sent to fight in the Vietnam War.

1967 *Homage to Marilyn Monroe* exhibition is held at the Sidney Janis Gallery.

1969 A major large-scale exhibition, or retrospective, is devoted to Oldenburg's work at the Museum of Modern Art in New York.

Neil Armstrong is the first man to walk on the Moon.

1974 The retrospective of Pop Art at the Whitney Museum of American Art in New York is seen by many to mark the end of the Pop Art movement.

1975 The last U.S. troops leave Vietnam following the war.

2001 The retrospective called *Les années Pop [The Pop Years]: 1956–1968* shows at the Pompidou Centre in Paris, France.

2007 *The Pop Art Portraits* exhibition opens at the National Portrait Gallery, London, U.K.

Glossary

abstract in art, not made to look like anything recognizable that we see in reality. Instead, abstract art uses shapes and/or colors to suggest a mood or idea.

Abstract Expressionism movement in art in the United States in the 1940s and 1950s, in which artists quickly and forcefully created abstract paintings, to express powerful emotions

airbrush hand-held paint sprayer, which artists use to spray a fine mist of paint onto a canvas

anti-art art shown in galleries or other normal displays that makes fun of serious art. Dadaism is a form of anti-art.

Benday dots dots used in a method of printing. Regular patterns of different-sized dots of color give different visual effects. For example, different colors of dots are overlapped to create other colors.

bronze metal that is an alloy of copper and tin, and sometimes other elements

brushstroke mark left by a brush loaded with paint. Brushstrokes differ in terms of their direction, texture, and the thickness of the paint.

Capitalist Realism German Pop Art movement of the early 1960s

cast shape or model made by pouring liquid clay or metal into a container and leaving it to harden

Cold War period of hostility between Western countries (the United States and Western Europe) and Communist countries (particularly the Soviet Union), from 1945 to 1990

commercial art art that is made for commercial (business) purposes, such as advertising or packaging

consumer society a modern society, such as the United States, where consumption—buying new things—is a major influence on people's lives

culture the customs, values, and attitudes of a particular society at a particular time and place

Dada art movement that started as a reaction to the horrors of World War I (1914–18). Dadaists used unusual objects and materials to shock viewers.

edition in printmaking, the number of identical prints an artist makes from one original plate

expressionist in the style of Expressionism. This is an art movement in which artists used bright colors, thick brushstrokes, and exaggerated shapes. They did this to express their feelings and to cause an emotional response in the viewer. Expressionist artists include Vincent van Gogh and Edvard Munch.

gestural marks marks in paintings, such as brushstrokes or drips of paint, that are signs of the strong movement and feelings with which the artist created the work

gradation smooth, gradual change from one color to another, or from color to no color

graphic designer person who has been trained in the art of combining text and illustrations, for example, in advertisements, magazines, or books

Happening artistic event, with audience participation, held in New York in the 1950s and onward

icon in art, an image or symbolic representation of a subject with religious or cultural significance. For example, Marilyn Monroe was made into an icon by many Pop artists.

impasto thick build-up of paint, to create texture

impersonal in art, showing no sign of the artist's personality. For example, smooth brushstrokes and lack of expressionism give this effect.

Impressionism art movement of the nineteenth century in which artists, such as Claude Monet, rapidly painted their impressions of the changing sunlight and color of scenes, especially outdoors

Independent Group London-based group of artists in the mid-1950s, interested in popular, mass culture

installation work of art made of different parts, in a particular space that has significance for the work. For example, Oldenburg's work *The Store* used lots of sculptures in a space made to look like a store.

movement trend in style, theme, or approach of art during a specific period

multiples repeated or copied artworks. These include the series of prints of the same subject created by Andy Warhol and the objects for sale in Claes Oldenburg's Pop store.

Optical (Op) Art type of art created in the 1960s by abstract artists who used painted lines and shapes to give an effect of movement

photomontage single image created by arranging multiple photographs together

Photorealism style of painting and sculpture where the works are created to look very realistic, like photographs

screen-printing technique for printing on surfaces by forcing ink through spaces in stretched fabric

squeegee tool with a flexible edge for scraping off or forcing liquid into spaces on a flat surface

street art art created in public spaces. Some street art is created on surfaces where art is not wanted, for example, graffiti on buildings. Other street art is encouraged, such as chalk artworks on sidewalks.

subject theme, topic, person, or object that an artist chooses for an image

superpower country, such as the United States or China, that affects the decisions and actions of governments of other countries. Superpowers have international power, for example, by having bigger armies or more money than other countries.

three-dimensional rounded, with height, width, and depth

two-dimensional flat, with height and width only

Find Out More

Useful websites

General sites on Pop Art and the history of modern art

www.metmuseum.org/toah/hm/11/hm11.htm
What types of art were being created around the world at the same time as Pop Art? The Metropolitan Museum of Art in New York has a website with a comprehensive timeline of Art History. You can click on different centuries on the timeline at the top, and then on different regions of the world map, to find out more.

www.tate.org.uk
Visit the Tate collection section of this website and you can check out biographies and selected images of any of the artists mentioned in this book. There are also descriptions of art movements.

www.artlex.com/ArtLex/a/abstractexpr.html
This is an online art dictionary. In the Index, click on "Pon–Pq" and scroll down until you reach Pop Art. There is a short description of the movement and then lots of thumbnails of Pop Art, which show the variety of work produced in this movement.

Sites featuring individual Pop artists

www.warhol.org
This is Andy Warhol's site, where you can see many examples of his art. Also, in the interactive section, you can learn about screen-printing by making your own in the style of Warhol.

www.lichtensteinfoundation.org/
This is Roy Lichtenstein's site. You can search all his images, by decade when they were produced, or by country and collection where they can be seen.

www.oldenburgvanbruggen.com/lsp.htm.
Here you can find photographs of Claes Oldenburg's large-scale sculptures, which he made in partnership with the Dutch artist Coosje van Bruggen.

www.ibiblio.org/wm/paint/auth/hockney
Here you can see some typical images by David Hockney, including two joiners.

www.jimrosenquist-artist.com
James Rosenquist's website features a detailed biography, which refers to his most famous paintings of the Pop years. Click on their names to see the paintings. The site also has a section devoted to his current work on a series called *The Speed of Light*, and a section listing galleries that show his work.

Websites with things to do

Have you ever edited photographs using Photoshop software? If so, you might be interested to try creating a Pop Art-style portrait following the instructions at:
www.melissaclifton.com/tutorial-popart.html
www.digitalartsonline.co.uk/tutorials/index.cfm?featureid=1468
http://princetonol.com/groups/iad/lessons/middle/connie-screen.htm

To make some art in the style of the street artist Keith Haring, and send some cards that feature him, visit:
www.haringkids.com

Would you shop for Pop? Visit www.othercriteria.com/index2.php to see works by Damien Hirst for sale and www.artofbrianjones.com/gallery/n_collages_gal.html for funny David Beckham collages.

Artists and movements to research

Pop artists were influenced by the art that was produced before them, just as later artists were influenced by the spirit of Pop Art. Why not extend your art studies by finding out more about artists and movements influenced by Pop Art? Use Google or any search engine on Internet Explorer, Netscape, or Mozilla to carry out your research.

Artists to research include Sigmar Polke, Gerhard Richter, Joseph Beuys, Juan Munoz, and Christo.

Movements to research include Arte Povera, Low-brow Art, Plop Art, Stuckism, and Neo-Dada.

More books to read

Demilly, Christian. *Pop Art* (Adventures in Art). New York: Prestel, 2007.

Dickens, Rose. *The Usborne Introduction to Modern Art* (Internet linked). Eveleth, MN: Usborne Books, 2005.

Grenberg, Jan and Jordan, Sandra. *Andy Warhol, Prince of Pop*. New York: Dell Laurel Leaf, 2007.

Hill, Laban Carrick. *America Dreaming: How Youth Changed America in the '60s*. Boston, MA: Little, Brown Young Readers, 2007.

Raimondo, Joyce. *Make it Pop!: Activities and Adventures in Pop Art* (Art Explorers). New York: Watson-Guptill, 2006.

Places to visit

Many galleries and museums have Pop Art, but here are a few with very strong collections including lots of varied pieces:

Andy Warhol Museum, Pittsburgh, PA

Museum Ludwig, Cologne, Germany

Museum of Modern Art, New York

Whitney Museum of American Art, New York

Wolverhampton Art Gallery, West Midlands, U.K.

Tate Gallery, London, U.K.

Index